Tessa Tries to
Hula Hoop

Concept by Amy Neel & Madison Wiggin

Written by Amy Neel

Illustrated by Valentina Esposito

WE MAKE FITNESS FUN!

www.MadAboutHoops.com

I can't believe it's finally here,
I wonder what I'll learn this year!
Here we go, the first day of third grade.
I see my teacher; she smiles and waves.

I take my seat as she starts to say,
"Tell me about yourselves today.
Tell me your name and one thing that you do,
a hobby or talent, what makes you, you?
Why don't we start with the first chair,
stand up tall when it's your turn to share."

I look ahead to count and see
how many people are in front of me.
Uh–oh, it's only THREE!

Gracie says can make a garden grow.
Sonia says she likes to sew.
Jeremy shares about gymnastics.
He showed us a flip, it was fantastic!

It's my turn, I get up from my seat.
I look at my teacher and start to speak:

"My name is Tessa but you can call me Tess.
When It comes to hobbies I've had no success.
I tried many things to discover my talent.
I've searched and I've scoured but still haven't found it."

"All of my friends have found their things,
but not me. I can't even sing!
Taya loves theater, it's easy to see,
but remembering those lines is not for me.
Hannah loves hockey. I tried that too,
but after one game I was frozen and blue."

"Blake loves to bake. Her treats are so sweet,
but when it comes to food I think I'll just eat.
Darrin can dance ballet and hip hop,
 but when I started to spin I just couldn't stop.
Sophie loves sports," I said as I started to sweat,
"but me, I still haven't found my thing yet."

I took a big breath but before I could speak
my teacher told me to take my seat.
"Tess," she said, "you'll find your thing,
but the bell is about to ring.
Just this once I'll let you slide,
now it's time to go outside."

Welcome Back!

What is your talent?

Recess 9:30
Lunch 11:30

That day at recess on the swing,
I saw a toy circle, sort of a ring.
I ran right over and scooped it up.
I gave it a spin but had no luck.
I tried again and then it once more,
 but my hula hoop just hit the floor.
Feeling defeated I was ready to quit,
but then I heard someone say, "You can do it!"

Harley the hooper came over to see.
Everyone knows she's the hula hoop queen.
I handed her the hoop and turned away,
I guess I won't find my thing today.
Before I could go she stopped me and asked,
"have you ever tried a hula hoop class?"
She said, "when I started I couldn't quite do it,
but after some practice, there's nothing to it!"

She showed me the proper way to stand
and how to push the hoop from my hand.
 She said, "start the hoop on your back
and spread your feet wide,
then move your hips from side to side."
Hooping wasn't easy, but it was starting to click,
and then Harley showed me some really cool tricks!

MAD ABOUT HOOPS

My family was so happy to hear me ask
if I could join Harley's hula Hoop class!
We practiced every day after school.
This hula hoop thing was pretty cool.
My hula hoop teacher says practice makes progress
and when the hoop falls, it's all part of the process.

My hula hooping gets better each day.
If my teacher asks again, I know just what to say:

My name is Tess and I've found my thing,
it's this little plastic ring.
If you're like me and feeling stuck,
my best advice is to never give up!
Just Take a deep breath and then regroup,
maybe try a hula hoop!

MAD ABOUT HOOPS

Tessa Tries to
Hula Hoop

Would you like to learn to hula hoop from professional hula hoopers at Mad About Hoops?

Scan this QR code to access your <u>FREE</u> hoop class!

Enter 'TESSA' at checkout

This book is dedicated to Taya and Tessa Neel and to our incredible Mad About Hoops students who inspire us every day. Always remember that hrough practice and a positive mindset, you can accomplish anything!

www.MadAboutHoops.com

Made in the USA
Coppell, TX
12 February 2021